PSYCHOSIS
A MEMOIR

Bethan Jenkins

Text copyright © Bethan Jenkins 2025
Design copyright © Chrissie Yeomans 2025
All rights reserved.

Bethan Jenkins has asserted her right under the Copyright, Designs and Patents Act 1988 to be identified as the author of this work.

No part of this book may be reprinted or reproduced or utilised in any form or by electronic, mechanical or any other means, now known or hereafter invented, including photocopying or recording, or in any information storage or retrieval system, without the permission in writing from the Publisher and Author.

First published 2025
by Rowanvale Books Ltd
The Gate
Keppoch Street
Roath
Cardiff
CF24 3JW
www.rowanvalebooks.com

A CIP catalogue record for this book is available from the British Library.
ISBN: 978-1-83584-061-0
eBook ISBN: 978-1-83584-062-7

Trigger Warning

This book contains discussion of depression, psychosis, possession, spirituality and conspiracy theories, which may be unsettling for some readers.

Disclaimer

I am in no way a doctor or medical professional. This book is based on my experience from my perspective, and the opinions shared and expressed are just that: my opinions.

Firstly, I want to say a huge thank you to you reading this book. I am truly so thankful for the chance to share my story and even more thankful for the chance to possibly broaden your awareness of a terrible mental health condition: psychosis.

It is my sincerest prayer that this book falls into the hands of someone that it could help in some way. That I can deliver this information in an easy-to-read format and that my views and the information provided throughout be truthful and, where applicable, scripturally sound. My focus and opinions throughout will be on psychosis and the nature of psychotic symptoms, so I ask that you not be disappointed at the promise of a little Christian content. If you are a Christian, I ask that you be open to my views and sympathetic to the events that I will share in this book. I will try my very best to describe the events I experienced clearly, but as the nature of psychosis is to be delusional, some of this content may not fully make sense. Please persevere.

Throughout this book, I will give some insight and helpful information about psychosis. I have also included a list of resources for those living in the UK in need of further help or advice. I will provide a collection of literature and websites that I'd recommend for those living with or supporting someone living with mental health conditions. You will find these resources near the back of the book.

In the beginning of this book, you will find my own personal story and experience with psychosis. Along with my experience, I have included one of my favourite psalms from the Holy Bible. A psalm which I hope will be of great consolation to you and help you reflect in your own walk of life.

Love, Bethan x

PSYCHOSIS

BREAKDOWNS AND BURNING QUESTIONS

For me, it started with questions... deep questions that not even Google could answer. It was mid-2019, and I'd started to ponder life and search for meaning to the mundane. I realised that most of the time I felt empty, unloved and unable to love others in a healthy manner.

I was unlucky enough to have had a string of unhealthy relationships. Three, to be exact. Two of which ended when I found both men looking to cheat on me through online dating websites, and one because of truly horrible narcissistic abuse. After enduring just a few months of this narcissistic abuse, I ended the relationship by waiting for the man to leave the country and then swiftly changing the locks to my house and moving his possessions into a storage container for him to collect upon his return. I plucked up the courage to get this done after I'd sought help from a counsellor named Rachel, who I found online. I explained my situation to her, and she helped me to recognise it was toxic, and so rather than confront him, possibly getting physically hurt in the process, I concocted this plan to get him out of my life efficiently. It broke my heart. Having to admit to another failed relationship shattered what was left of my confident 'I am loveable' facade.

I soon after realised that materialism didn't matter to me as much anymore, and I was even tired of travelling. I always returned unsettled and wanting more from life. In hindsight, I was becoming depressed.

I started questioning myself, too, and what had led me to so many unhealthy relationships. Why did I choose such destructive relationships? Why did I live life this way? Why had this guy verbally abused me and thrown his weight around? Was it my fault in some way? What was the point of it all anyway?

Relationships?

Life?

A HIGHER LOVE

These questions led me to a comfy seat on rattan furniture in a heated conservatory in west Wales. The home of that same counsellor named Rachel. She had bouncy red hair, a soft smile and an attitude to match. We chatted about how I felt and how I felt about the people around me, my relationships and my hurts. I spilled out my heart as tears painted my cheeks. Drop by drop, I began to feel lighter. The recognition she gave me and the space to sob was, as it turned out, just what I needed.

The view helped too. Rachel's home had a staggering view of beautiful Welsh countryside, just the ticket for an aching heart.

During our session, we spoke about how others had hurt me, how I had hurt others and what my expectations were from our sessions. I remember one significant thing that I said during this meeting, and that was: 'I wish there was a book that told me how to live life.' She replied earnestly that there wasn't, and she looked really sad to break that news to me.

I drove the forty minutes back to my grey, humble terraced home in weary silence, the window down and the breeze cool on my damp cheeks.

I returned to Rachel's every couple of weeks for the next four or five months. Every time I left feeling freer than the last, like each tear was breaking a link in the chains that held me in sadness. We spoke about attachment styles, childhood trauma, my hurts and joys in life, my expectations from others, and she posed great questions to me that got me thinking more about how my emotions were driving my actions. Until finally, one day, those strained chains binding me to sadness just broke.

I had woken up to get ready to leave for another session and found myself singing 'Amazing Grace' whilst at the stovetop stirring my porridge. I felt like I was present for the first time in my life, like I'd finally processed my significant past traumas. That morning, after our final session, I even sang my way home! Belting out a sloppy rendition of 'Higher Love' on repeat, windows down and the volume up, I thought to myself, *The song is right—there must be a higher love, something greater than ourselves, something worthwhile*. I decided then and there that I believed in a god.

On reaching my home, I sat down with a cup of tea to think some more on why I now believed in a god and what kind of god I was deciding to believe in. I realised that this profound change in my emotions from counselling had made me feel like there must be a god; after all, it was like someone had simply flicked a switch and now I felt like I was being given a second chance at life.

After thinking for some time, I decided that I believed in a god who was watching me all the time. A god who knew all of my thoughts. A god who knew all of my secrets. Having read some of the New Testament as a child in school and learned that the biblical God was all-knowing, I decided that was the only God I could believe in. So, still in the spirit of sharing my secrets, I decided to use God as my counsel now.

I rifled through my house for a notepad and pen and started writing down all of the things I could remember doing wrong in life. If I had felt good whilst starting, this list quickly humbled me. I found it hard to even write some of the things I was remembering. I didn't want to own up to them, and I cringed just at the thought. I even laughed nervously at the thought that God already knew everything I'd ever done, and even knew when I was lying or softening the truth. So, I was brutal! I wrote down everything I could remember—

everything from lying, stealing, cheating, to hurting others and more.

Unfortunately, it was a very long list. I am, as it turns out, like all of us, a perpetual sinner. And it was an incomplete list, I might add. Of course, I will never remember all the millions of times I have sinned against God, but I gave it my very best attempt with the knowledge that I had.

MEDITATION

I had recently started listening to a podcast by ex-Hollywood actor and TV presenter Russell Brand, on which he spoke about all things philosophical. I was enjoying it as a nightly routine. So that night, having just finished up one of his podcasts, I decided to embark on a philosophy degree to satiate my thirst for something bigger than myself, when something else caught my attention. The next podcast on Russell's list was a guided meditation with Deepak Chopra (a well-known New Age teacher). I'd never heard of him, and I'd never taken part in a guided meditation before, but I had always heard that meditation was good for mental health, so without hesitation I settled into what I imagined to be the perfect meditation pose and pressed play.

Well, it went as any first meditation session is bound to go. I couldn't cope with my own thoughts as I tried to watch them go by without judgement like Deepak said. He spoke about being the viewer behind the self, and I was surprised to find that I understood what he meant. My mind was a busy mess, but I longed for the silence that meditation could offer me. So, I tried the next night and the next night and the next.

ENTER PSYCHOSIS

Only, one of the evenings that followed, whilst I lay on my bed searching for that silence, that space beyond, that ever-watching presence beyond my thoughts, something else found me. I experienced what I could only describe as energy climbing my legs. A physical sensation that came from my big toe and wound its way up my left leg like a snake slowly coiling its prey. I shook my leg violently, trying to stop its ascent. It went just as quick as it came.

I started to shiver, my legs jerked uncontrollably, and I felt the urge to double down on the toilet. Vomit burnt my throat. I spent the rest of the night pacing around my bathroom, cold feet padding along tile-effect vinyl. I didn't feel tired at all, which is something I'd later come to learn could be a sign of mania.

The next day, I didn't eat a thing; hunger and thirst evaded me all day until I found myself parched and frazzled, lying on my bed in the evening. I lay there staring at the ceiling for a time until I drifted into a space of silence, of steady breathing, somewhere between awake and asleep, and I felt it again. That feeling was back. It climbed my legs, this time fast in a straight procession to my stomach, where I felt it pulse like a steady, rhythmic heartbeat.

I opened my eyes in shock and was dumbstruck to find stars covering my ceiling. Real stars! Only they couldn't be real, could they? They shone there like someone had taken a can opener to the roof of my house and opened up the ceiling for me to bask under the night sky.

I peered at the doorway, where I saw what appeared to be a pair of hands floating in the air in prayer position. A very real pair of hands. I instinctively 'knew' to copy the hands, and I held my hands in prayer position over that beating in my stomach. As I did this the hands disappeared and the shadows in the room began to follow my breathing. As I breathed in, the shadows would spread across the night sky displayed above me, and as I breathed out, they would recede, and the stars would shine brightly over me once again.

That's when the energy began to climb my body again, this time into my throat. It climbed until I could feel it on the very back of my tongue. I gagged and tried to open my mouth, but the energy snapped my mouth shut again. My jaw locked. I was terrified; my mouth was dry and my throat felt like sandpaper, and there was something there in my throat. I felt something cool hit my tongue and my mouth reacted with saliva.

I sat bolt upright, gasping for breath. The sandpaper feeling had gone. My mouth opened and I could swallow again without pain. My body... the room... everything was back to normal. What *was* that?!

I did what most millennials would do and reached for my phone. But instead of calling someone for help, I sat there in the dark, frantically googling my symptoms. It didn't take very long at all until I was thrust into the history of Hinduism and Buddhism, and I was half an hour deep into it when I found it. Google said it was a spiritual awakening! Or, more specifically, what is called a kundalini awakening. An awakening that comes after a period of deep questioning. A time where energy spontaneously climbs your body and awakens or activates your chakras (energy points in the body) one by one, and it comes with a whole host of possible symptoms. The exact things I was experiencing!

That's it! I thought. A spontaneous kundalini awakening! Just to confirm my findings, I then stumbled upon forums of people who had experienced the exact same thing as I was experiencing. Perfect! Now I knew what to do… the forums all said that I just needed to ride it out until it reached the crown of my head. Once it starts working on you, there is no way to stop it until it completes its journey. Great—there was more to come…

A WORLD TO SAVE

The next evening, I turned out the light early, prepared to get some sleep, hoping that the forums were wrong, although there was no mistaking my experiences.

That's when the orbs of light came. Hundreds of them, in all different sizes, floating around me as I sat in the darkness on my bed. Mostly they were just bright white lights, but some were blue, and some were various shades of purple. Some of them formed bright white lines of light around me, and I sat there frozen to the spot, trying not to breathe. Fight, flight or freeze, right? I definitely froze.

I'd never seen orbs before, but I had heard about them many times on a show called *Most Haunted,* where people went to haunted buildings hunting ghosts. I was equally amazed and terrified. I was in a room full of spirits!

The music started to play right about then. Toto's 'Africa' started to play as if on the radio, but I didn't have a radio in my room. It played loudly and unmistakably, as if playing inside my ears. I closed my eyes, and right there behind my eyelids, I saw the continent of Africa as clear as day. I knew what I had to do... Get on a plane to Africa to save the world! That was the most obvious explanation I could think of. I just knew it was true! I had images running through my head of me driving to Bristol Airport and leaving the car door open and the engine running in my haste to get through the terminal. More images of me being greeted off the plane by people who already knew who I was. And I knew deep in my soul that I somehow wouldn't survive the trip; I knew one hundred percent that I wouldn't be coming back and that I needed to die there in order to save the entire world from hunger and devastation. I didn't know how it would happen, but I did know that it must happen, and what was I waiting for? I had a world to save!

A quick check on Google told me that the first flight was in just a few days' time. Perfect—I'd have just enough time to tell Rachel everything that was happening with me.

WIDE EYES AND LIES

Sitting there on Rachel's sofa, I explained, wide-eyed and full of awe, how I'd received these messages to fly to Africa and save the world from suffering. Her eyes opened just a fraction more, and I had the sense that she was not taking my news as positively as I'd hoped. She tried to calm me down by listening to me intently. I begged her to meditate so she would know the truth, so she too would activate this dormant energy in her body and start to have visions and messages, just like I had. She agreed to try to meditate and let me leave her conservatory office with an awkward, pitying smile. I assumed it would be our final conversation.

In the car on the way home, I sang a song from the musical *Hadestown*. Over and over again, I listened to it, feeling a shiver ripple through me every time. I thought I had received a message from the lyrics. When I switched it off and turned on the radio, I realised the radio was talking to me! Certain words and sentences would jump out like messages directed just at me. I thought to myself that not everybody has this happen to them, so I must truly be 'chosen'. Chosen to save the world.

Ring ring! When I got home, the phone rang and it was Rachel. She promptly told me, in the softest but firmest voice she had, that she had made a doctor's appointment for me to attend that afternoon. I told her that the doctor would think I was crazy and that all of this stuff was really happening to me. I didn't want to go, but now that the doctor had been alerted, I had no choice; it would look odd if I didn't attend.

Outside the doctor's surgery, I mustered up my greatest poker face and breathed deeply whilst checking myself in the mirror.

I entered the doctor's office and was greeted by a female doctor. She asked me general questions about how I was feeling, and I told her that I was feeling great. Which was truthful—I was. I was high on adrenaline rushes and my fear system was fully activated, which was leaving me buzzing.

Then, however, she asked me if I was seeing things. Was I seeing anything odd? Hallucinations? 'No,' I said, 'definitely not.' And I was only half telling the truth, because I didn't think they were hallucinations. I thought they were real, without a shadow of a doubt, one hundred percent real. I had seen them clearly with my own eyes, after all.

The doctor told me, 'Well, you look normal,' and sent me away with a smile.

I'd passed. I'd lied, but I'd passed.

SHAME AND PSYCHOSIS

Over the next few days, my high came down, and I realised that I must have had what the internet called a kundalini psychosis. It was a kind of psychosis, but not the kind that needs medication to improve, I read.

The visions had stopped, and I was feeling back to myself. I felt ashamed. Ashamed of the things

I'd thought whilst I was experiencing this kundalini psychosis. *I must never tell anyone,* I thought.

I visited Rachel for one final session. I felt so nervous to face her again. I felt so foolish. But I also still believed that I had experienced a spiritual awakening and that if the doctor had been told the truth of what I had seen then I would be locked up in a mental institute.

Rachel was rightly curious about what I had said to the doctor. I told her that I had lied. I insisted then and there to Rachel that I had indeed experienced a spiritual awakening and that I did recognise it had resulted in me displaying psychotic symptoms, but I was better now! I explained how I felt grounded and the visions had stopped and so had the messages on the radio.

However unlikely it may seem in hindsight, Rachel let me leave her conservatory office that day with a warm smile and a bunch of well wishes for the future. She told me that her door was always open, and then, without further conversation, I turned to leave and clambered into my SEAT Ibiza.

ANGELS, SPIRIT GUIDES & GIFTS

I started to meditate again. Meditation was the key to this, apparently. The internet said if I meditated every day, I would activate my gifts of clairvoyance (seeing in the spirit) and clairaudience (hearing in the spirit). I'd be able to hear my spirit guides and they would help me through this awakening. But first I had to have reiki (the laying on of hands) to help the energy flow through my body unobstructed to avoid another spiritual psychosis.

I went to the local crystal and reiki shop to ask for help (a shop that I didn't know had been there for a year prior to this, so it felt like kismet) after finding out online that I needed crystals and reiki therapy to get me through a spiritual awakening. The lady there, Daria, said I had a lovely energy and proceeded to lay her hands over my body as I lay on the therapy bed. The room made me feel dizzy, but that could have been my nerves. The room was full of crystals and pictures of angels, and the lights were turned down dim. Daria said that I had an old soul and very angelic energy. I asked her what that meant and she said, 'Oh, you can contact the angels.'

Pffft, I thought. *Angels? Angels don't exist here... do they*? Daria assured me that they do indeed exist and that if I was to light a candle and meditate and call on them, I would connect with them very easily. They would be like spirit guides for me for the rest of my life.

Wow! I thought. I was living in a dream. A dream where I was excited and marginally terrified all at the same time.

I returned home, lit a candle and burned some incense. I settled into my most comfortable meditation pose, cross-legged on the floor beside the candle. Once my heartbeat settled, I called out, 'Are you there?'

A rustling in the corner sent my heart dancing again, and I saw that a plastic carrier had fallen off the nearby dining table. Phew! It was just a carrier bag. So, I let my heartbeat resume a steady pace and I called out again.

Ting! This time a bell rang somewhere in the corner of the room in response. I asked again, and before I could even finish my question, what sounded like huge wings started to beat in my right ear! So strongly and so loudly that I imagined the hair on my head blowing to the left with every beat. Wow!

This lasted for around twenty seconds. Once it finished, I quickly blew out the candle, spat on the incense and collected myself, scared, into my bedroom.

What had just happened? Could it be? An actual angel had just visited me?!

From then on, I spoke with Daria many times. She told me that if I dedicated myself to meditation, I would connect easily with my angels and would receive gifts. Gifts of clairaudience, clairvoyance, clairsentience and claircognizance. She explained to me how to protect myself in the spiritual realm by imagining a white light surrounding myself and my home, and by using crystals for protection. She told me I could also call on famous angels like Archangel Michael and Archangel Gabriel, and they would bring me their strengths. Each angel had different strengths and could help in different ways.

One night, I searched for books online to study to help me get accustomed to this new way of life. Books on angels, reiki, soulmates, twin flames, meditation, spirit guides and crystals. I was amazed at the options available to me. A whole world of spiritual knowledge that I didn't even know existed! I got stuck in and soon found myself buying spiritual aids so I could contact spirits and ask for guidance.

ANGEL NUMBERS AND SIGNS

In the books, I learned about angel numbers. Angel numbers are repeating numbers that pop up in everyday life that the angels use to communicate with us... apparently. These can be times, car number plates, house numbers, phone numbers, bank account numbers, etc. I was awestruck! I had been noticing repeated numbers on my phone clock for weeks now. Every time I had seen them, I had taken them as a bad omen, but now I knew they were just messages from angels. Perfect—things were looking up. My scary spiritual psychosis was in the past and my new spiritual life had begun.

One day, during meditation, I asked the spirits if I should get a deck of tarot cards to be better able to receive guidance from them. I had been meditating in the car, and after receiving no direct answer, I started the engine and drove off. The first car to pull out in front of me had 'TRT' at the end of the registration number, and I took it as meaning 'Tarot'—and a resounding yes from my spirit guides!

It was like this for months; I would see patterns in numbers and signs in all sorts of normal happenings in life.

One time I was walking down a street near to my home when I spotted a page that had been torn from a book lying in the grass beside me. I glanced at the page and noticed the title 'Take the Long Way Home'. So, I did. I took a detour and took the long way back to my home! On the way, I found my recycling bags, which had been blown away one blustery night three nights prior, and I thought, *YES! Thank you spirit guides for your signs!*

It didn't occur to me that this could be coincidence. I had come to understand that coincidences didn't exist. Our lives were all fully thought out and constructed for our individual needs by our spirit guides and angels.

So, I lived that way for months. Throwing caution to the wind and following every 'sign' or 'synchronicity' I came across.

VISIONS AND VOICES

During my daily meditations, I would receive guidance in the form of thought, as voices in my head. They would either sound like my own voice or, very rarely, like someone else's voice entirely. I took this as my angels and spirit guides conversing with me.

I would also feel the spirits touching me. They would gently touch my face during meditation, and one time I even felt them tap all ten fingers and thumbs across my forehead. But mostly it was subtle. I'd feel my forehead tingle, which was, I was told, my third eye opening.

One time I was at the stovetop, stirring my evening meal, when geometric shapes flooded my field of vision. I could still see the room through them, but they were like a web of patterns over my sight. It lasted a good ten minutes. I was so used to it by then that I remember carrying on stirring and serving up dinner as if nothing was happening at all. It was all just a regular evening for a regular modern-day witch, and that was what I would come to call myself and take pride in.

During these months, I had bouts where this so-called kundalini energy would awaken in my body. I'd see it lighting up my brow like I had a head torch strapped to my forehead, or bursting through my hands and making my wrists arch backwards in the process. All sorts of weird and wonderful things would happen to me, each one making me feel more powerful and with more purpose in life. I was living according to my New Age purpose. My purpose was now to follow guidance to unlock my true potential as a human being.

Soon, during my Google phases throughout the day, I started stumbling upon a whole plethora of conspiracy theories. In particular, alien conspiracy theories and how the government was covering alien operations up. I can't wholeheartedly start to put these theories into words for fear that they may trigger something in me. Something that could start off delusional thinking again. Because that is what they did. I might have been delusional before—whilst I was busy trying to save the world, conversing with angels and spirit guides daily—but I had yet to see the worst of it.

STARSEEDS AND ONENESS

I had been seeing an alien-type face on the wall in my bedroom for months. I also saw her when I closed my eyes. I thought she was just another spirit guide, but she looked different to the others. I googled her characteristics, and I came across a drawing of a woman who looked exactly like her. She was a Pleiadian from the Pleiades! So, the conspiracy theories were true, and—I was conversing with an extraterrestrial from another galaxy! Wow!

There was a lot more to this world than I'd once realised, and to confirm this for me was another forum online. A forum where the people called themselves starseeds. Starseeds were described as people who had souls that had lived other lives in different galaxies. They too had tales of conversing with Pleiadians and other extraterrestrial races. Me being me, I took this to another level. I ordered books on starseeds and even joined an online group where we all shared stories in real time via Zoom. The Soul Light Collective. I felt connected to each and every person on the call because they were all talking exactly the same way as I was. They were sharing stories too, some more crazy than mine. We laughed, we meditated and we cried together. We shared life together, and it was the best feeling, finding people who could validate this strange experience I'd been having so far very much alone.

    I'd always felt alone, in fact; even as a small child, I'd been plagued by loneliness. A feeling that couldn't be erased even by the busiest of rooms. So, for the first time in my life, I felt a part of something much bigger than myself, and I ate it up. It temporarily made me feel a sense of purpose and a sense of togetherness. After all, the New Age does teach that 'we are all one'. One with nature, one with each other and one with God. I was finally feeling that oneness—or so I thought.

I learned so much from the group. I learned how to use sage to 'clear my energy' by burning it until it smoked and then sweeping it around my body. I learned how to heal my ancestral lineage using psychosomatic work and magic spells. I learned all about twin flames, soulmates and reincarnation. I used crystals to meditate with daily, one of my favourite being a starseed crystal which had little notches on one side of it that were apparently downloaded information from an ancient civilisation called Atlantis. I spent a small fortune on crystal necklaces and collected feathers as I believed they were tokens gifted to me by the angels. I celebrated Samhain, Eostre and summer solstice by dancing around my room, burning sage and meditating on live Zoom calls with my new starseed friends. I learned all about the law of attraction and the laws of karma and dharma. I practiced qigong and yoga like it was going out of fashion and believed in praying to many different deities. Basically, if you can think of it, you can pray to it: the ocean, the moon, Archangel Michael, the Goddess of the Sun, Mother Mary, etc. The list is truly endless.

In the year that followed, I did much of the same whilst also living my everyday normal life. I'd fit in meditation every day without fail, sometimes meditating for up to two hours. I received visions through meditating. Like still pictures or movies in my mind's eye.

I followed guidance and talked to my 'spirit guides' about everything. I'd feel the spirits entering the room—the lights would even start to flicker when I meditated—and I'd hear the spirits' voices in my head. I'd see their faces in the carpets and walls. I'd read my own future through tarot cards and I'd do readings for my new psychic friends. Life was anything but simple, and I must admit I was enjoying it.

BURNOUT

Yet I came to a point where I was tired. Tired of meditating, tired of chasing guidance and tired of thinking I was attaining 'secret wisdom', because it never amounted to anything. It was exhausting actually. I was tired of the 'spirits' that plagued me every night with voices in my head, tired of the conspiracy theories... Dare I say that I just wanted to be normal!

I was also still lacking something. I realised that all of the spiritual gifts in the world would not fill that emptiness that I had inside of me. Of course, now I know why... I didn't know the promises of a sovereign God.

THE STRANGER ON THE BEACH

In the summer of 2021, the sun strong in the sky, I walked through my local sand dunes to the closest beach, as I'd quite frequently do. After spending quite some time on that beach, I noticed the tide was coming in pretty close, so I packed up my bags and dragged them away from the shoreline.

A passing stranger saw me struggling with my half-packed bags and offered to help me. I declined the offer, but she stood firm next to me. As we clambered up powdery sand towards the nearest dune, she introduced herself as Hannah. Hannah was bright as a button and much older than me; she was also, as it turned out, very hungry. She asked if she could sit with me whilst she ate. I agreed to the company, and we found ourselves eating and staring at the ocean together.

I told Hannah that she was very youthful in her ways, and she replied, 'That's thanks to God.'

Oh, here we go, I thought. *Another Bible basher that obviously doesn't know the spiritual realm like I do.* I humoured her and smiled.

She went on: 'I used to do reiki and wear only purple like a right witch, but now I feel free. God has given me purpose.'

She smiled a content smile, but my ears pricked. Did she say reiki? I replied that I had also done reiki and read tarot cards.

She made a *hmm* sound and said no more on the matter.

We sat there together for a while before we decided to head back to the car park.

Hannah wrote down her number on a piece of paper and said, 'I've wished I'd handed my number out to someone before and I didn't and I regretted it, so I'm handing it to you now. I'd love to stay in touch if you'd like to.'

There was no way of that happening; she was the opposite of the people I'd come to know as my friends in the starseed community. Although, I was curious about her reiki past and why—and moreover how—she would turn away from something like this just to follow a biblical God. To be restrained and restricted by biblical teachings. It made no sense to me, as the New Age had no rules to follow except 'positive intentions always'.

I graciously accepted the piece of paper with her number scribbled on it and decided I'd never need to use it.

DEMONS

That evening, I remained curious about how someone could turn from this spiritual way of life and enter into a life of following biblical teachings. Yet I didn't even know what the Bible taught. I mean, I knew that it said wives must submit to their husbands, because people would often throw that point up as a reason not to follow the Bible, and I knew that a man named Jesus died on a cross for the sins of the world, but I didn't understand it. To me, following New Age teachings, Jesus was an ascended master who loved everyone just as they are and taught 'Christ consciousness' to people during meditation. I didn't get it.

And what do we do with things we don't understand? We google them! So I entered into Google 'what are the commandments?' and soon found myself perusing through a book of the Bible called Deuteronomy.

Now, if you know the book of Deuteronomy then you'll know what I found. If you don't happen to know this book then I'll tell you it is full of warnings against worshipping idols, practising divination, witchcraft and occult practices.

Let no one be found among you who sacrifices their son or daughter in the fire, who practices divination or sorcery, interprets omens, engages in witchcraft, or casts spells, or who is a medium or spiritist or who consults the dead. Anyone who does these things is detestable to the Lord; because of these same detestable practices the Lord your God will drive out the nations before you. You must be blameless before the Lord.

Deuteronomy 18:9-13 (NIV)

The shock on my face would have been apparent if there'd been anyone there to see it. Not only was I practising the majority of those things, but God actually said that I was 'detestable' to Him.

I kept searching and I came across a woman that I'd seen before in my searches of angels. Doreen Virtue. A woman who had been deep into occult New Age practices and sold millions of copies of books and angel card decks worldwide. She had, just a few years prior, turned away from all association with New Age practices and given her life to Jesus! Yes—to Jesus! She was now dedicating her time to Bible readings, churches and studying theology, and her social media was full of warnings against New Age practices. (New Age practices include everything I had been involved in this far.) And to top it off, the icing on the cake, was that she called these angels that I had been so accustomed to talking to DEMONS. Yes, demons! Demonic spirits.

My heart sank to my gut and all rationale plummeted from my mind at the word 'demon'. I frantically searched for more information. I found the book of Corinthians.

...for even Satan himself masquerades as an angel of light.

Corinthians 11:13 (NIV)

There it was. These bright light angels I'd been talking to were actually demons. My skin crawled at the thought of demons touching me and whispering in my ear. I sat there in horror at the thought that I'd been unknowingly giving Satan permission to rule my life, and most of all that I was detestable to God! That in my search for God I'd become so far removed from Him that my all-knowing, all-seeing God now found me detestable in His sight.

With that, I picked up the phone and texted the only person I could think of texting for help. Hannah from the beach. I asked her if we could meet up as soon as possible and she replied with tomorrow at 11 a.m.

I soothed myself by telling myself that Hannah would know what to do, I'd just have to make it through one more night with a head full of demons. But, I thought, they had always been so friendly before now, right? So I was hopeful I'd just sleep off my fear, wake up fresh and see Hannah; we'd stop all of this noise in my head for good tomorrow and I'd be back to normal before sunset. No problems, right?

That night, I couldn't sleep a wink. The bright blue lights I'd usually see floating around the room had turned a bright shade of red and came up close to my face. I started to have repetitive negative thoughts that felt like they were almost placed into my mind by an outside force, and my thoughts were being stolen from me when I tried in vain to pray against them. I'd start to say the Lord's Prayer, just the way I remembered it from school, and my thoughts seemed to get stolen mid-sentence and replaced by bad words. It felt like a battle going on in my mind. I was too afraid of the dark to leave the room to go to the toilet, so I held it until morning and stayed awake all night with the light on in the bedroom.

With the break of day came an increase of bravery, and I washed and dressed with ease and rigour. *I'll be free of this stuff by tonight*, I told myself.

THE BOOK OF LIFE AND A BONFIRE

That morning, as I pulled into the college where I'd agreed to meet Hannah, tyres crunching up a gravelly driveway flanked by trees, I felt a sense of peace. When Hannah met me and led me into the garden, all my worries felt out of place. I took in the surroundings. Large lawns bordered by summer flowers, a large, towering building that stood as the college and a picnic blanket that Hannah was now spreading out on the lush green grass. I perched on the blanket, waiting for the general chit-chat to be over with so I could unleash my experience on her and she could help me fix this thing.

That time came quicker than expected as I tried to rush through my story, missing out chunks in the process. Only, this woman didn't look shocked. She quickly assessed what I was saying and told me that it was true that these spirits were demonic and there was a spiritual battle going on between light and darkness.

She said, 'Let's pray together over it.'

So, we closed our eyes under the strong summer sun, and she prayed for me whilst I agreed to everything she was saying with my whole heart.

I told her about the angel numbers following me around and the signs and asked how I could make them stop. She said that I would just stop noticing them after a while and that it would all be ok. She asked me what number I saw the most often and I said 42. So, she opened her large-print Bible and read Psalm 42 out to me in the heat of midday.

As soon as she started to read 'as the deer pants for the streams of water, so my soul pants for you, O God...' I burst into tears. She continued, and I felt a pull on my heart and the rolling tears just kept coming.

Every word of this psalm spoke to me. 'Deep calls to deep in the roar of your waterfalls...' Every word like ointment for an aching, scared soul, and I puddled into the mat beneath me.

I told her that it was Him this entire time; that I had been looking for something/someone and He'd actually been leading me to Him this entire time, but I had been looking in the wrong places. A busy fool. She went on to explain more about who Jesus is and shared the Good News with me. She gave me a hug and told me I could always pray to Jesus, and He would answer.

So, right there, on the spot, I said yes to giving my life to Jesus. It felt like coming home. Like everything that had happened to me had happened for this reason of coming home, of laying up my tattered hat on the rugged cross of Jesus' sacrifice. Home.

I had heard the story of Jesus in a school religious studies classroom years prior, but only then did I finally understand that a man named Jesus didn't just sacrifice

Himself on the cross to save mankind from their sins, but He died for me! A perpetual sinner! For me and my sinful ways! He died so that I may be seen without blemish and brought home to the Creator.

In this moment, I was overcome with emotion. I was home, and the demons I thought I was experiencing seemed so small next to a mighty God.

I returned to my mother's house with a spring in my step and asked her if I could stay there for a while. She agreed that this was for the best. She was very concerned for me, as any mother would be. I disclosed to her only a very small fraction of what had happened and told her that it was ok because Hannah knew that prayer could help me, and I'd given my life to Jesus. My mum was shocked, but I'm not sure of what exactly her feelings were at the time as I was solely focused on myself. I remember her crying for me as I explained with such emotion what had happened in the garden, and the concerned motherly look on her face.

I asked her if she had a Bible in the house, and she dug out an old New King James Bible for me to look at. I started to study the New Testament and learn passages that I could use during times of spiritual warfare, just as

Hannah had explained to me to do. I didn't want to be caught like a rabbit in the headlights like I had been the previous night.

We started a bonfire out the back garden, my mother, stepdad and I, and I burned up all of my occult books and spiritual aids, then turned my focus to the one book that mattered. The Bible. I had finally found a book that told me how to live a peaceful life. It was time for a fresh start.

DELIVERANCE AND DEMONIC POSSESSION

That night, I went to bed dreading the long night ahead. Sure enough, that night and every night after it, I would experience thick energy entering the room. I'd feel it tingle on my hands and against my entire body. The red lights would flash near my face as if in warning, and when I tried to fall asleep, I'd have visions of black entities with red eyes. Where my spirit guides had been, now demons were in their place. The aliens on the walls were still there, only now they looked menacing, and although I prayed against them what felt like every ten minutes, they didn't disappear.

I met up with Hannah and another lady every Friday from then on and we prayed against everything I had done. All of it. Bit by bit. It was excruciating for me as every time I saw them I was giving them just a snippet of my experience, when what I really wanted was to let it all out, pray against it all and then be done with it. God would take it all away. But Hannah assured me that I had to remember each thing I had done and ask God for forgiveness from it; only then would it go away.

This I know now not to be true. We humans are not even able to remember our previous day accurately, let alone remember and account for every sin we've ever committed in life. But I was at the mercy of the knowledge of others.

One day, Hannah called me up to the college and told me that she thought I was possessed. She said she had thought it previously but didn't think I was strong enough to deal with it at the time. My gut felt full of magnets at the word 'possessed'. She said that she'd been reading up on deliverance ministry and knew just what to do. So, after much deliberation on my part, sitting under a gazebo tent on the lawn of the college with the door flaps raging in the evening wind, we began. She told me to relax as much as possible and allow anything that wanted to come out to come out.

She spoke directly to the demon and ordered it to come out in the name of Jesus. My mouth contorted into a smile and a deep, nervous laugh came out. I was taken aback and quickly spoke to her, saying I didn't want to do this anymore. She assured me I was ok and that I had the mind of Christ and I could get through this.

So, we finished up. Nothing else happened, and soon I was back in the car blasting the *Psalms* album by Shane & Shane, trying to forget the whole thing. Only, it didn't work. The deliverance wasn't enough! The thoughts and the visions of lights just kept coming.

We vowed to try again with a pastor at the local Pentecostal church. And we did try again. This time, I roared like a dragon because I was letting out what felt right, and afterwards, I felt freer than I had before. So, we decided to do one final deliverance and pencilled it in our diaries.

Life went on, and by day I enjoyed life within a church, slowly learning more about Jesus and the new friendships that it brought. By night, I put up with little sleep and these terrible things that plagued me.

THE LION IN THE CAMPSITE

Come late July, some people from the church decided to book to go camping in August in Newquay near the beach, and I was sold on the idea. I loved camping, I loved walking, and I loved the beach, so when they asked me, it was a resounding yes. The only thing was, it clashed with my next deliverance session. I knew that I needed deliverance because this stuff kept happening to me at night, but I also decided that God had me protected and I deserved a little fun. I knew there was the possibility that a rough night was ahead of me, but I went camping anyway. It couldn't be much worse than any other night, could it?

The first night camping, I met and spoke with a kind couple outside their tent over a cup of filtered coffee. The conversation went well until suddenly I felt like my senses had been heightened and everything they said seemed to now drip with negative intention. Although now I forget what they said, I know that it was just general chatter that was not ill intentioned. But at the time, I had full-body chills from the way I felt about them. So, I got up and moved my entire tent away from theirs to avoid being near them.

As I walked away from them and toward the small crowd collected by the campfire, I saw one of the little boys crying in a Spider-Man costume. His eyes looked abnormally large and his features were grim and contorted. I knew then there was something seriously wrong with me.

I stayed away from the crowd for the rest of the evening, and I actually have lost time, where I don't remember a portion of the evening. I do remember begging my friend, the church pastor, to be baptised. I had been told by Hannah that some people were delivered of demons when they were baptised, and so I was desperate. I didn't tell him that was the reason why I wanted to be baptised, and he didn't know everything about my experience like Hannah did. He declined my request to be baptised as he thought it would be best to do it as a church. I was gutted.

All I remember next is that one of the kind ladies there was comforting me and passed me her phone. When I said hello down the phone, Hannah's voice came back at me. Hannah had been told that everyone was concerned about me, and she was ringing to check I was doing ok. I kept repeating that I didn't know why everyone looked so sad around me. But all I was really thinking was that these nice people were going to burn me alive if I got into that tent. The paranoia had started.

I knew with my entire being that I was going to die in that tent. After a lot of coaxing, I finally got into the tent, but once I was zipped in, I just stayed awake the entire night. At one point, I heard a real lion circling around the tent, snuffling against the other side of the thin fabric with a low growl. In my head I thought of the Bible verse, Peter 1:8: **'Be alert and of sober mind. Your enemy the devil prowls around like a roaring lion looking for someone to devour.'** (NIV)

I was so terrified that I urinated right there in my sleeping bag. It was that real to me.

I heard the roaring of the crashing ocean in the background of the quiet night, and I thought what I heard was a faint horn blaring in the night and a beast coming out of the sea. I thought of Revelation 13:1: **'I saw a beast coming out of the sea. It had ten horns and seven heads, with ten crowns on its horns, and on each head a blasphemous name.'** (NIV)

I saw images of everyone who was camping being hurried into the nearby barn without me (we were camping on a farm), and Matthew 3:10 came to my mind: **'He will gather His wheat into the barn, but the chaff He will burn up with unquenchable fire.'** (NIV) I had visions of me wrapped in melting molten fabric as the field burned up around me.

I urinated with fear again. I had never been so terrified in my whole entire life. I spent the night praying and saying sorry over and over again.

Come break of day, I left the tent and quickly changed my clothes and mopped up the mess with my sleeping bag. I took the sleeping bag through the field towards my car, where I was going to place it in the boot, and I planned to leave after breakfast.

Only, unexpectedly, Hannah was standing by my car. She had decided to take the two-hour drive to come and get me because everyone, including herself, was very concerned about me. One of the women there hugged me, and as she did, she began to cry for me. I gave her a hug and told her I was going to be ok and that I knew what I had to do. I knew I had to do the deliverance again, and so did Hannah.

She said, 'Are you ready?'

I said yes and we bundled into her little car, and she drove me home. On the way, I kept unbuckling my seatbelt because I had visions of a beast coming in through the windscreen and carrying me away and I didn't want anyone else in the car to be harmed. Hannah kept buckling it back in. She gave me a pillow to rest on and offered me a milk and honey biscuit to eat. I saw that it was milk and honey and I rejected it, thinking that I couldn't offend God by eating something He promises to His loved ones.

My mind was officially gone.

DELUSIONS AND DEMONS

We arrived outside my mother's house, and I paused before going inside. Hannah said she didn't want to stick around because the demon in my mother would react to her presence, so she left before my mother came to the door.

The bell rang and it was so loud to me that it was deafening. I had full-body shivers. Since Hannah had said that my mum had demons inside her too, I became really scared.

When my mum came to the door, her eyes were large, black and round, and her features over-exaggerated, just like the music video for Soundgarden's 'Black Hole

Sun'. (If you don't know it then I'd recommend you look it up and watch it to get an idea of what things can look like for somebody suffering hallucinations.)

We were in the lounge, and my sister was there with the baby. She said that my face was bright red, so I checked in the mirror, and it was a true shade of crimson. I was flushed. It dawned on me then that I was being taken over by this demon that was living inside of me.

My sister offered to let me hold the baby, and I declined out of fear that the demon would take over and I'd hurt the baby. When my sister chatted with my mother, she laughed, and it sounded like an obnoxious cackle and her face contorted into a demonic face. I was seeing demons in everyone. Yet I stayed quiet and pretended that I didn't see them, because if they knew that I knew they were demons, I thought all hell would break loose.

I went upstairs to get away from the demons, and I had all sorts of beliefs running through my mind: that my family were going to let the gas out of the oven and blow the house up with me in it, that the devil wanted my soul and wouldn't stop until he had me, that the demons were going to hurt me and take my family, that my family was going to harm me, that I was reincarnated from the Israelite times and my family was full of demons and they were out to get me, that I was a fallen angel and I was getting my just punishment—the list goes on, and each belief was one hundred percent true to me. The strongest belief of all was that the end of the world was impending, and Jesus was going to take all Christians to be with Him.

There was no question that all of these beliefs could live in my mind simultaneously and they could all be true. I was, in hindsight, absolutely falling apart.

ASSESSMENTS, TELEPATHY & DEHYDRATION

I was admitted for assessment at my local mental health clinic. Whitewashed walls, two sofas and a separate room with a lockable steel door and a red bean-bag bed in the centre. I now know it was a seclusion room, but at the time I thought I'd been kidnapped.

I remember staring out of the window in the nearby room waiting to see the sky change to darkness, which would signify the end of the world. I also thought there was a conspiracy against me and that I was a fallen angel, and they were going to 'deal' with me.

I remember them taking me into a room with a psychiatric doctor for an assessment. The doctor asked if I thought people could read my mind, and up until that moment I hadn't thought so, but now that he had said this it put the thought in my head. I didn't answer him, but I now believed that they were reading my mind. Suddenly, my head was full of voices that were sabotaging me. I couldn't control them. They were calling people names and being abusive toward the staff. I spent my time trying to block them out or repeatedly apologising to people via telepathy.

This was how I communicated at this time; I started to talk to people through my thoughts. For example, a male doctor asked me what I was thinking, and, in my head, I replied, *You know what I am thinking! But I can't say it aloud, so please stop all of this!*

Of course, he couldn't read my mind, but without a shred of doubt I thought that he could. He never did answer me, but he did smile, and I took it as confirmation that he knew what I was thinking and that he just thought it was fun to play games with me.

I was kept in that room for what felt like weeks but was actually only a few days. I actually said to one of the women that I had been there for a week and they hadn't offered me a shower yet. She insisted I'd only been there for two nights, but I didn't believe her. I had lost all sense of time.

The staff changed over every hour, and one of the male staff came into the room with a book titled *A Time for Mercy*. I took it as a reference to me and what was in store for me when they were allowed to have their own way. I imagined them beating me and burying me alive.

I took a sip of water at the same moment I was reading through a printout that they had given me which stated that they could give me medication without my consent. I gasped aloud. I stared at the water bottle, imagining that these people had drugged it, and I noticed the label: 'Princes Gate' water. (Bear with me on this one.) The realisation hit me... that I was the prince. The Prince of Darkness. I was a fallen angel. Satan incarnate. They were going to drug me and shackle me in chains and bury me alive. Bury me alive with a giant snake to get me back for being the serpent in the Garden of Eden! This was my 'gate' to hell, the 'Prince's Gate'.

The label read 'filtered by rocks, bottled by us'. 'Us' I thought must mean the NHS. I suddenly realised that the NHS had a rainbow as their logo. But the rainbow was also God's promise to never flood the world to rid the world of sin again! Now I thought I really was Satan and the NHS were taking me out of the world for God!

I didn't speak a word of this out loud, only in my head. The entire time, I spoke in my head. From that moment, I stopped drinking water. I thought that the water would keep me alive for longer when they buried me, as water represents life in the Bible. So, I starved and dehydrated myself from this moment.

I stayed that way—parched, terrified and clutching at my head to stop my thoughts—until the nurse coaxed me into accepting a lorazepam tablet and I passed out on the giant red bean-bag bed, probably, in the most part, from exhaustion.

GENERAL HOSPITAL

After some time of starvation and dehydration, I was transferred to a general hospital where they dressed me in a backless hospital gown and intended to hook me up to a drip for rehydration.

They first took my vital signs and concluded that my blood pressure was dangerously low and so were my blood sugars. They poked me with needles, and I protested, saying that they were taking the last of my blood. The blood came out thick and dry, my lips were sticking to my teeth from lack of saliva and I found it impossible to cry. I was finally drying up. I refused their offers of food because I wanted to die peacefully and quickly. I didn't want the food to prolong my life and I certainly didn't want it to make me live forever, like I feared it would!

A doctor came into the room with a clipboard and asked me a few serious questions.

He asked me if I was on a hunger strike for protest reasons.

'No,' I answered.

He asked me if I knew that I would certainly die if I didn't have any food or drink.

I answered in my head this time: *I don't want to live forever*. I couldn't answer him verbally because if they knew that I knew about the snake and the live burial they might do it sooner and I wouldn't get a chance to die.

Before I knew it, nurses were in the room talking to my chaperones, who then pinned me to the bed as my legs flailed and a needle pierced my skin.

'No!' I shouted over and over.

I could barely put up a struggle because I had no energy or strength and I weighed just 50kg. I started to feel drowsy very quickly and my limbs went limp.

They explained to me how they had to insert a feeding tube into my nose and down my throat and that if I struggled it would make the situation worse than it needed to be. I saw the bag of 'feed' in a plump nurse's hands. She smiled at me a smile that seemed to say 'I'm sorry.' None of the nurses looked happy to be there and they all looked very truly sorry for what they had to do to me.

I wept a tearless cry. I groaned and thrashed and kept my eyes on the bag of 'feed'.

After some struggle, they managed to insert the tube into my nose and down to my stomach, and they transferred me for an X-ray to ensure that it was in the right place. I lost count of the number of times we went through this process, because every time they weren't looking, I lay down and quietly pulled the tube out of my nose to let the 'feed' spill out under the covers and onto the sheets of my bed. Each time they didn't notice that I had done it until the bag had finished. They pulled back the covers to find me covered in mocha-flavour feed.

When I saw the name 'Fortisip' on the feed bag, I thought to myself that forty was the number of days Jesus was tested by Satan in the wilderness. I was sure then that I had forty days of this until they buried me alive. I thought that everything had significance, and I was terrified. I'd do everything I could to sabotage them so I could die peacefully.

They decided it was best to fit me with a bridle that tied the tube to my nose. If I pulled on it, the bridle would tug at my septum and be really painful. I tried a few times to yank it out but the pain was awful. Eventually, though, I found a part of the tube that wasn't bound by the bridle and I tugged on it, and the tube came all the way out. I remember feeling such relief at this. In my mind, every time the tube slipped out of my nose I was getting closer to death but every drop of Fortisip that entered my body brought me closer to health, and for many reasons I would do everything I could to die.

Eventually they weighed me, and I had increased in weight. Healthy enough to leave but only on the strict instruction that I was to drink prescribed Fortisip every day. I agreed, to get out of there, but a drop of Fortisip never crossed my lips.

SECTIONED

In October 2021, at 31 years old, still in my backless hospital gown, unwashed and half starved, I was transferred to a mental health hospital in the East Midlands.

I remember the arched rainbow over the doorway as the car pulled up to the entrance, and it sent a shiver down my spine. The rainbow. God's promise. As I thought that I was Satan, I thought that this place must be my final destination.

I was welcomed by a couple of people, and I think that they explained where I was. I can't to this day recall what they said because I spent the whole time pleading with them in my head, thinking that they could read my mind.

I do remember Francis. Francis came through the door and told me he was a manager. He told the others he would 'take it from here'. He ushered me forward through a wooden door and into a long corridor. The corridor had a number of locked, windowed doors along it, each leading to the next, and along the sides of the corridor were other doors with blacked-out windows. Francis was walking in the direction of the locked doors, and as he opened the first one with a key fob, I realised that he was waiting for me to follow him. I had no choice. My body was trembling and I wanted to turn back, but there were only locked doors. The corridors were all empty. It was just me and Francis. Not a soul in sight.

We continued down the corridor until we reached the last door, which had no window, where my eyes landed on a sign and my heart bottomed out.

'Welcome to Eden,' Francis said as I stepped through the door, and it crashed closed and locked behind me.

I couldn't believe this place was called Eden! It just consolidated all of my beliefs. This was it! The serpent (me) finally back in the garden! Eden… my final destination.

I stayed there in Eden, a medium secure ward, receiving treatment for 18 months. There was a boxed TV in the corner, some wipe-clean green and deep purple sofas, and an office to the back of the room where staff sat behind a large plexiglass window typing up their notes and observing us patients.

There were eight patients on the ward including myself. We each had our own room with en-suite down a corridor just off the living area, and there was a dining area with a food hatch where we were all to gather at mealtimes. Lunch at 12 and dinner at 5 p.m.

Two members of staff had to follow me around and observe me for a while whilst I 'settled in'. This level of observation quickly dropped to one member of staff, which I was glad of as their conversations had proved difficult for me to hear, because I swore they were always talking about me.

A couple of days into my stay on Eden ward, the doctor decided it best to mix medication in the form of antipsychotics into my Fortisip feed that they administered via nasogastric tube. I was given this medication against my will. I flailed around and fought them every mealtime and ripped the tube out of my nose whenever I could. They sounded the alarm every time, and up to ten staff would respond to the call, taking it in turns to pin me to the chair to be fed. I'd have two people on my legs, two on my arms and one person holding my head up. Until, one evening, they decided to administer the antipsychotic olanzapine in injection form.

The nurse warned me that this would happen if I kept refusing tablets, so I insisted that it was my right to be given information on the drug. The nurse printed out an information leaflet for me, and I frantically read it as he prepared the needle. One of the side effects I noticed was hallucinations or worsening of psychotic symptoms. I protested but I was pinned down and administered olanzapine via IM.

The world swirled and I started to hallucinate immediately afterwards. Bright lights crowded my vision before I crashed and passed out on the bed.

When I woke up, I remember being surprised that I wasn't dead or buried alive. It was the first time that the word 'hallucinations' resonated with me just a little, that maybe what I was experiencing could be a distortion of some kind.

MEDICATION AND BREAKTHROUGH

From then on, they continued to mix olanzapine tablets with the liquid feed they were giving me, and each day afterwards I became a little more compliant until eventually I was sitting down peacefully, accepting the tube down my nose without fuss. This was partly down to how ravenous I was becoming. It turns out that they had decided on giving me olanzapine because it would increase my appetite as well as treat the psychosis. After three months of starvation, my desire to satiate my hunger was finally outweighing my fearful thoughts and my thoughts of suicide.

One day, late October, I decided to try a jelly sweet that someone had left in my room. The flavour was incredible! My dry, parched mouth wasn't used to tasting anymore, and one taste led to me finishing off the small bag of sweets. Later that day, I joined the other patients on the ward for dinner and ate half of a cheese and beetroot sandwich. The medication was doing its job, regardless of my sabotage attempts.

The medication had a list of side effects, the most common being drowsiness. I slept the days away; I was unable to function properly, and when I was awake I was tired in all of the ways someone could be tired. Emotionally, mentally, physically and spiritually tired. I was also riddled with bouts of anxiety during the day. Anxiety that made me feel like crawling out of my own skin. But there was no doubt the medication was working for me. My mind was slowly starting to heal. I even started to take the oral medication prescribed to me: 20mg olanzapine in dissolvable tablet form once daily.

The anxiety became so overwhelming that I begged the nurse to help me with it. I begged for more medication! They said they could prescribe me an anti-anxiety medication in the form of pregabalin, and they also added a PRN medication to my chart (a medication that I could take whenever I felt overwhelmed), 2mg clonazepam when required. After a week of taking the pregabalin, I had the terrible side effect of a swollen, painful stomach and had to stop taking it. From then on, whenever I felt completely overwhelmed, I would ask for clonazepam and would space out on the sofa in the day area or on my bed until I fell asleep.

I was also prescribed an antidepressant, 20mg escitalopram once daily. Luckily, I never had any side effects from the antidepressant, and from what I can fathom it must have helped as I was not quite suicidal anymore, even though I would pray for God to take me to heaven most nights.

PSYCHOLOGY, PSYCHICS AND THE PARANORMAL

The ward psychologist had introduced herself to me shortly before I started eating again, and we had started having weekly check-ins. During these sessions, she explained to me how she had seen many cases of psychosis, and she slowly and carefully explained to me some of the common symptoms. These were roughly the following:

Delusional thinking – Where someone has an unshakeable belief in something untrue. Like believing they are the queen, they can save the world, or some organisation is out to kill or harm them.

Paranoia – The persistent feeling that other people are 'out to get you'.

Hallucinations – Where someone hears, sees, smells, tastes or feels things that do not exist outside of their mind.

Depression – A low mood which lasts a long time. It usually includes feelings of hopelessness and difficulty finding pleasure in everyday life.

I noticed that these symptoms matched up to some of my own experiences, but even though I made the connections, I found it very hard to put my knowledge of spiritual matters aside and pick up this new knowledge. I assumed she was lying to me or didn't know the full truth. This is a common symptom in psychosis sufferers. Most sufferers don't believe they are unwell. I still believed strongly in my experiences. I believed strongly that my 'visions' of orbs and aliens had been one hundred percent real and could not be classed as 'hallucinations'.

However, as our meetings went on, I couldn't deny the fact that these 'visions' didn't happen to me anymore. In fact, since I'd started steadily being administered the olanzapine, I hadn't had any more 'visions' at all.

This realisation was slow growing; it didn't happen overnight, but it did happen. At some point in my treatment the scales tipped, and I came to the conclusion that I had in fact experienced hallucinations.

This conclusion birthed new questions. If I had experienced psychosis from the very beginning of my journey, then how had so many people on my path been experiencing the same things? Was everybody that I'd met experiencing psychosis too? And what about the medley of literature there is online about these phenomena? Or had the psychosis started when I learned that these phenomena had been demonic entities? Had my mind finally had too much information to handle and responded in a chemical reaction, causing an imbalance of some kind? Did the fear response cause my mental breakdown, or had my whole experience been psychosis? Had I started off psychic and swiftly moved to psychotic?

With these burning questions at the forefront of my mind, I opened up the conversation with the psychologist. I wanted to know her thoughts on spiritual gifts and how she thought people could live their whole lives thinking they were speaking to spirit guides and following spiritual guidance. Were these people all wrong? Were they all experiencing psychosis? What was the difference between those people and me? How could we have had such wildly similar experiences and yet ultimately such wildly different outcomes?

Instead of asking all of these questions, I posed a single question which I don't remember at this time. I do, however, remember her answer. She said something which has stuck with me: 'It's ok if someone believes there's fairies at the bottom of the garden, but when those fairies are telling you to harm yourself it becomes a problem.' In other words, it's not a problem until it becomes one. For me, it had become a big problem.

We came to understand that people who have psychic experiences have a controlled entry and exit into and out of these states, whereas for a person suffering from psychosis, these states are largely unwanted and uncontrolled. Often, a psychic has a better grip on reality, whereas someone in the throes of psychosis has a limited grip on reality. Where psychic experiences usually have life-enhancing consequences, psychotic experiences usually result in social and behavioural deterioration. In effect, it's not the experience itself but how one's brain copes with the experience that defines it.

Through my own research, I have since learnt that it is thought that psychic and psychosis are on a continuum, with 'normal' on one end and full-blown schizophrenia on the other. One essay I found online is 'Mysticism and Madness' (Greenberg et al., 1992), which is a very interesting paper to read through.

Another paper I found online titled 'Spiritual aspects of psychosis and recovery' by Dr Susan Mitchell states:

> Some people view their madness as a spiritual journey. But can religious or spiritual

experiences be distinguished from psychotic ones? A number of studies have found it impossible to differentiate between mystical experiences and psychosis solely on the basis of phenomenological description. (Greenberg et al. 1992, Jackson & Fulford 1997, Saver & Rabin 1997.)

The same paper also states:

What seems to be important is the way in which the psychotic phenomena are embedded in the values or beliefs of a person: 'It is not what you believe but how you believe it'. Distress and unwanted preoccupations characterise psychosis, whereas spiritual experiences may be sought after and are more often associated with positive life changes (Greenberg 1992, Lukoff 1985). The kinship and difference between mystical and psychotic states is captured in essence here by Jelaluddin Rumi, the 13th Century Persian Sufi (Barks, 1993):

The mystic dances in the sun,
Hearing music others don't.
'Insanity', they say, those others.

If so, it's a very gentle,
nourishing sort.

How much of my experience was down to the 'paranormal', I do not know. The lights flickering, a book flying off the shelf, the bell ringing in the corner of the room and other events that can't be explained under the bracket of mental illness definitely occurred. There is no doubt about that. However, all of the visions, sounds and physical feelings of hands on my body can also be explained as visual, audial and tactile hallucinations. The only thing I know for certain is that I suffered from a psychotic break, and it was the scariest thing I've ever had the misfortune of experiencing. Any questioning of the paranormal pales against the importance of me knowing that fact. I do not care about the existence of the paranormal as much as I care about the seriousness of my mental health condition.

FAITH AND REFLECTIONS

My psychosis seemed to have started from depression and exhaustion, and would have started in late 2019 when I had that first full-blown psychotic episode which I called a spiritual awakening. I had been through a period of consistently not sleeping before this journey unfolded, and I had been seriously depressed whilst working through my traumas with Rachel, my counsellor, in those early days. Both these things can be common triggers for psychosis to occur, and as it went untreated, it just got progressively worse.

Importantly, the psychologist and I spoke about my faith. In early hospitalisation, I had doubted the love of God and His ability to save me. All of my focus had been on how God didn't deliver me from my 'demons' and that I must not have been faithful enough or loved enough to be healed or delivered. I had been scouring textbooks during my psychosis and looking for hidden meanings in the Bible to explain why I thought I was going to hell, and one day, as my condition improved, I realised that I hadn't found any! What I read was grace, forgiveness and redemption from sin and suffering for those in Christ Jesus.

Therefore there is now no condemnation for those in Christ Jesus, because through Christ Jesus the law of the spirit that gives life has set you free from the law of sin and death.

Romans 8:1 (NIV)

One thing is for sure: I could never abandon my motivation to have faith in God.

So, we discussed how I could move on with faith whilst also keeping my head healthy and my mind well. This is so important. The Bible is full of stories of demons, which was one thing I had to forget about for a while in order to improve mentally. The thought of demonic oppression and demonic possession leading us away from eternal salvation in Jesus is absolutely terrifying, especially to someone who is mentally unwell. Beliefs can easily be twisted when suffering from psychosis, as I learned the hard way.

In Christianity, there is a section of misinformed people who want to deliver others of demons when they present symptoms of a mental health disorder. I also succumbed to this way of thinking during the throes of illness. I do believe that Jesus delivered people of unclean spirits and that the same can be done today; I mean, if man can influence man so easily then I see no reason that man can't be influenced or taken over by unclean spirits. But I admit that I am not qualified to say one way or the other. I do, however, believe in sickness and mental illness more than I ever have done.

What I do know is that, from experience, **we should treat the mind first**, and this often involves specialist therapies and psychiatric medication. I know now that I needed to get my brain into a chemical balance to even be able to begin to discern what I thought was the truth. All it did to hear the truth spoken to me during psychosis was add to the delusional thinking.

The truth was that I didn't have a demon. I was seriously unwell. I had turned to the Church for help and support, and unfortunately it made matters worse. The Church should be a place we can turn to for help with any struggles we may encounter in life, and I'm convinced that if all churches were willing to receive training and provide information on mental health conditions that it could become just that. A safe place for everyone.

Getting to know mental health conditions instead of demonising them is the first step. By doing this, we are showing God's love through our actions towards people who are struggling and are in need of our help and support. Whether that support be going for a walk with them, taking them to an appointment, prayer or referring them to a medical professional. It is so important to gain mental clarity and sweep out the distortions using medication before instilling faith into people by sharing the news of a loving God.

One thing is for sure: now that I am well, I could never give up on Jesus, and now that I am reading the Bible and Christian textbooks again, for the first time with a healthy mind, I couldn't ever have imagined a more loving God.

DELIVERANCE

God delivered me from my 'demons'—that is, mental illness. Not in an immediate 'one fell swoop', but profoundly just the same. My appearance during the throes of illness compared to now is a stark contrast. God set my deliverance pathway through hospitalisation and professional care, and He brought me mental clarity.

It wasn't as magical as it may sound; in fact, it was far, far from it. I had raging, angry questions about why a loving God had created mental sickness anyway. Why didn't He save me and everyone else from the darkness of mental illness? Some nights I didn't pray, and some nights my prayers were very dark and I begged for death to overcome me. There were times I listened to worship music and sang quietly through my tears, and times that I managed to actually find peace in God's promises of forgiveness from sin.

What I found very helpful was finding things to be thankful for. Gratitude is a great way to counteract anxiety and depression. I start my prayers most nights with a list of things I am thankful for. It can be hard to find anything at first, but I'd remind you to not overlook the seemingly insignificant things like being able to brush your teeth that day, get dressed that morning or take a short walk. I'd also recommend that you don't overlook the essentials like having a warm bed, a hot meal, a steaming shower or money to purchase what you needed that day.

In the Bible, it explains that gratitude to God can overcome anxieties and bring you a sense of peace.

I believe this to be true for everyone. If you are not a believer then this can be a simple pen-and-paper list of things that happened during the day that you can be thankful for, or even saying thank you out loud for things will help.

Paul writes in Philippians 4:6: **'do not be anxious about anything, but in every situation, by prayer and petition, with thanksgiving present your requests to God. And the peace of God, which transcends all understanding, will guard your hearts and your minds in Christ Jesus.'** (NIV)

MEDICATION, STIGMA & SIDE EFFECTS

My view on medication has completely changed, and I now see it as a tool to fix a sick body. A sick mind. Is it perfect? Not at all. But is it beneficial and can it help quality of life? Yes, definitely. Can medication be a strong rebuke for mental 'demons' in a modern-day hectic stressful world? I'm living proof.

Of course, people have varying degrees of success with psychiatric medication and it can be an incredibly tough journey. There is still much stigma around mental health illness, and although most people don't think twice about reaching for a paracetamol when they have a headache, there is a lot of shame that comes on a person when they are prescribed something to help them mentally.

For me, that shame comes with the word 'antipsychotic'. We all know how the term 'psychotic'—or mostly 'psycho'—is used to describe someone who is 'crazy', 'mad' or 'unstable'. I can't count the number of times I've heard the term 'psycho ex-girlfriend/boyfriend' used for someone who portrays delusions or strange, extreme or manipulative behaviours. It is generally used as a derogative word or to offend someone who is exhibiting unstable characteristics. It's an insult. There is even a modern secular song that sings about a woman being 'sweet but psycho'.

This stigma makes it hard for people who are suffering from symptoms to accept medication. Psychiatric medication, along with other therapies, is a blessing even though it's not perfect, and it is my hope that over time we will see less shame associated with taking medication for mental health.

What I've witnessed is that it can take time for each person to find a medication that works for them with few side effects, and of course, depending on the diagnosis, it is not a case of 'one tablet fixes everything'. Some of the girls on my ward, for example, as side effects of medication, have shakes and tremors, wet the bed frequently and have major weight gain from increased appetite and slow metabolism. They can still have delusional thoughts, bouts of self-harm, depression and mania even though they are medicated. I have been unfortunate enough to suffer from dizziness, sleepiness, mental fog and weight gain. In the time I've been in hospital, I have doubled in weight, and at one point I couldn't function because of the constant mental fog from the medication olanzapine.

I spoke with the doctor about this, and he created a plan for me to transition to another antipsychotic medication: 20mg of aripiprazole once daily. This medication has so far only come along with one side effect for me and seems to be working just fine. This side effect is heartburn, which I take a daily dose of omeprazole to manage. Aside from the heartburn, I have had great success with aripiprazole. I no longer have a mental fog hanging over me and I no longer feel overwhelmingly tired in the daytime.

I'm considered one of the lucky ones on the ward because I only take three tablets a day. Most other patients are on morning meds, lunchtime meds and nighttime meds to control their symptoms.

I'd like to address that there are a lot of Christians who believe that by taking medication you are putting your faith in worldly things when your faith should be put in God's ability to miraculously heal. I would say that a pill doesn't substitute prayer, but God works through many means. God has put it in people's hearts to become doctors and to create medicines that can help us in our times of need, and I think they should be viewed as the blessings they are.

Take 1 Timothy 5:23. Paul writes to Timothy: **'stop drinking only water, and use a little wine because of your stomach and your frequent illnesses.'** (NIV)

This advice to mix a little wine with his water suggests that Timothy may have stopped taking wine to avoid falling into temptation of sin, i.e. avoiding worldly things. However, in his letter, Paul is encouraging Timothy to take up a little wine, not for pleasure or satisfying the flesh, but for healing.

Timothy is not being disobedient to God or obedient to sin and the world; he is simply using other God-provided means to heal his own ailments. It is like this with medication. Taking medication does not make your faith in God redundant or mean that you are less faithful than others. It makes you no more reliant on the ways of the world and no less reliant on God.

Jesus Himself recognised that the sick needed doctors. In Matthew 9:13, He says: **'it is not the healthy that need a doctor, but the sick.'** (NIV)

DIAGNOSIS: DEPRESSION

This leads me to today. I am still in hospital three years on from being admitted. I am now 34 years old. I have been diagnosed with severe depression with psychotic symptoms.

Before this sudden onset of psychosis, I had never suffered with self-harm, hallucinations or delusional thinking. I didn't take drugs or drink alcohol. It is thought that it could be a one-off episode, albeit a long episode, of psychosis. There is no way to know for certain that it won't happen again, so they are still observing me, although I am stable and have been for a little while now.

In 2023, I moved to another ward where I managed to improve enough mentally to gain unescorted leave in my local area. The road to recovery has been long and sometimes tedious. Time moves at a snail's pace in hospital, and I am three years removed from what the staff here like to refer to as 'the community', aka the place that the rest of the population lives: everywhere that isn't a mental health facility.

I still suffer from depression, which is down to personal family losses and my circumstances, but I have hope in the hard times. I have learned to honour the depression and feel it.

Oh boy, have I ever felt it. Depression is a cruel thief of joy. It is a bottomless pit of darkness. Numbness accompanies major depression, and when I'm depressed I can while away hours staring at the wall with a blank, numb mind. 'Sadness' cannot effectively describe what is felt in depression. When I cry, I feel a break in my depression, a moment where I'm able to actually feel something. So I welcome sadness as much as I welcome joy.

However, there are more days where I feel joy now. Days where the depression doesn't come in full force and joy is able to break through the surface. I make sure I get up and get dressed every day, and I utilise methods of coping that I've learned from psychology sessions, and it's proving very effective in treating my depression.

WELLNESS AND THE WEATHER

I have come to understand that wellness involves the ability to be your own therapist, and I have learned a great deal from three years of therapy. Wellness is not something you can buy from an Instagram wellness guru or the like; it's the ability to go through the ups and downs of life and navigate them to the best of your ability.

I have learned many practical skills in psychology. I generally use CBT (cognitive behavioural therapy) on a daily basis and weed my own mental garden regularly, applying what I know psychologically to be true. I've undertaken CFT (compassion focused therapy) to help build self-compassion while moving forward with a previous mental health diagnosis. I still have help from my psychologist weekly and she is still here to talk me through my grief and despair at my experience.

My mental needs are very well met here in hospital, but I hope to move on to 'the community' again soon.

Three years in hospital takes its toll on a person. Importantly, I always have access to a great friend from my hometown whenever I need a good chat, and I have been blessed with incredibly supportive family and friends. Isn't that the most important thing? We need people to keep well.

Proverbs 12:23 says: **'anxiety weighs down the heart, but a kind word cheers it up.'** (NIV)

This is so true! **Other people will always play an important part in our healing.** Going through that pain with others is important. Life will always hurt in some way, but it's where we place our hope that is important. Surround yourself with people who hope and encourage others to hope too. Because hope is the hardest thing to have when dealing with a mental health condition.

Galatians 6:2 says to: **'carry each other's burdens, and in this way you will fulfil the law of Christ.'** (NIV) This means that we should share our struggles with others, even if we don't want to. **Always tell someone! Do not isolate yourself** due to mental health concerns, as isolation will make it worse. The more people who know, the better, as they can support you and even pray for you. Your honesty will give them a chance to show compassion. On the other hand, if you are on the receiving end and someone shares with you that they are struggling with mental health concerns, it is especially important to thank them for sharing their struggles with you. Thank them, pray for them and always follow up with them. If you can, make the time to just be there for them or ask them out for food or a coffee. Show them that they aren't alone.

One of my favourite analogies from my time with my psychologist has to be 'The Weather and the Sky'. It reads: 'Your observing self is like the sky. Thoughts and feelings are like the weather. The weather changes continually, but no matter how bad it gets, it cannot harm the sky in any way. The mightiest thunderstorm, the most turbulent hurricane, the most severe winter blizzard—these things cannot hurt or harm the sky. And no matter how bad the weather, the sky always has room for it—and sooner or later the weather always changes.' As Christians, we can go one step further and know that God created us to withstand all emotions, just like the sky was created to hold all of the changing weather.

LIFE INSIDE AN INSTITUTION AND INJUSTICE

Living in a mental health facility has been an eye-opener and a shocking plunge into the extremes of mental illness. In my time here, I have seen people tie ligatures, women split their heads open on walls and people swallow objects that are not meant to be ingested. I have smelled the extent of illness as people who are severely depressed refuse to shower or take care of personal hygiene. When I first arrived here, I myself didn't bathe or brush my teeth for three whole months! I couldn't bear to wash myself, so all the skin on my legs and feet was flaking off.

I have witnessed first-hand the lengths that women will go to, to harm themselves or even to try to take their own lives. These are daughters, friends, sisters, aunts and mothers. Every one of them has a relationship to someone who at one time was unable to take care of them. Or, in rare instances, when they are disowned from their families and have only the clothes on their backs, they have the help of the healthcare workers to fall back on for support. I have met women who have been in the services for 20-plus years and women who arrived at the tender age of 18 from children's services, only to be thrust into a ward of nine fully grown, unwell adults. I have heard their experiences and been there to witness some of the most vulnerable times of their lives, and I can't help but look at each of them and know how much better off they would be with a hope in God.

I pray for everyone, of course. In fact, if I am thankful for one thing in these past three years (other than the care I've received), it has to be the people I've met and been able to bless with prayer that they may have otherwise never had. On Eden ward, I used to read the psalms to a young lady with a personality disorder every time she was stressed or upset. I have been able to share my faith with other service users openly and delve into the conversations that it leads to. Not always pleasant conversations, but welcome conversations, nonetheless.

I've made great friends on the ward and found others that have been through the same delusional ways of thinking as I have. Some healthcare workers are absolutely fantastic at their job and are a credit to the hospital. I've met a hospital chaplain, some great occupational therapists and a lovely healthcare worker that have been really good 'friends' of mine during my stay here.

However, there is still a big gap in mental healthcare, and I have seen many an injustice. I have witnessed healthcare workers verbally abusing service users, ignoring patients and their needs, and I've even heard of a staff member praying over someone who was experiencing full-body shakes and delusional, paranoid thinking. The patient shook more violently out of fear of possible demons in her body and vomited all over the floor. I can't help but feel passionate about this after my own experience with mental health and so-called 'demonic possession'. If that had been onstage in a church that does deliverance ministry and the person had vomited out of fear, they would call it a success. But this wasn't a success. **Being sensitive to mental health illness instead of demonising it is so important, even for us Christians. Especially for us Christians.** We must always be considerate of the effects our actions and words are having on a person, even if our actions are well intentioned. **Indirectly praying for someone with mental health struggles can be a more considerate way of supporting them, as this way you also protect their dignity.** Whatever we do to support someone with mental illness, we should do with gentleness and kindness.

MENTAL ILLNESS IS NOT DEMONIC POSSESSION

With the rise of Christian TikTok and Instagram has come the rise of filmed deliverance services. I have seen some for myself, and it does seem that the recipients were freed from demonic possession in the name of Jesus. However, after my own experience, I can safely say that it is not always what it seems when such emotion is involved.

I don't claim to know the answers and I can't speak for the thousands of people who have been delivered in such a way and claim to be living a peaceful life of freedom in Christ. I am here, however, to say that **mental illness is real**. Mental illness is not demonic possession. Mental illness needs to be treated as an illness.

Of course, God can deliver us of all illness, including mental illness, but sometimes He wants us to seek out other means than miracles. Not because He can't do it, but because His miracle lies in another stage of our healing. For me, His miracle is in the fact that I've made it through to the other side of sanity. He set my path through doctors and nurses that had the knowledge to treat me. He walked with me through the shadows, even when I begged Him for death, and He led me to a place of healing where I am able to speak up for other people who are in the shadows too. God doesn't promise to spare us all illness and affliction; His promise is to faithfully walk with us should we become afflicted or ill. He does this by giving us hope when we turn to Him.

So, if you have tried deliverance and it hasn't worked, or you think you may be suffering from a mental health condition or any of the symptoms we discuss in this book, I want you to know that **you are far from alone** and there are people, including myself, that have struggled with mental health conditions too. **There are great doctors, nurses and clinicians who daily choose to put their energy into trying to help people who are suffering from mental health concerns. Use their services!** And most important of all, there is a loving God with you always, even when you feel most alone.

INSIGHT AND STATISTICS

It is my biggest hope that mental health gets its moment. Through this book, I want to open up the door to conversations about mental health. The brain is the most complex organ in the body and there is much we don't understand about mental health conditions.

In recent years, social media has erupted with people claiming that we need to take care of our mental health using techniques like deep breathing and mindfulness. Which is all fantastic advice, it truly is, but I'd love to see more representation of why we do this. Why we look after our own minds, and the signs and symptoms we need to look out for in our spouses, family members and friends who could be becoming mentally unwell.

Quite simply, mental health is more than taking baths, lighting candles and getting an early night. It is indeed all of those things, sometimes, but the reasons behind us doing it are varied and diverse. I have met people diagnosed with schizoaffective disorder, paranoid schizophrenia, bipolar disorder and various personality disorders, and people who have experienced psychosis like me. **We should look after our mental health because these illnesses can happen to anyone.** Depression is one of the most well-known mental health concerns of our day, and as I learned, it can lead to a full-blown psychotic episode.

In fact, any big troublesome or traumatic life event can lead to someone experiencing a psychotic episode.

Black, white, old, young, Christian, Buddhist, Muslim, etc., **psychosis doesn't discriminate.** In fact, 1 in 4 people in England will experience a mental health problem of some kind each year, according to Mind.org.uk. In any given week in England, 3 in 100 people are actually diagnosed with depression, and 8 in 100 are diagnosed with mixed anxiety and depression.

Although self-harm and suicidal thoughts aren't mental health diagnoses, they can be symptoms of diagnosed or undiagnosed mental illness. Shockingly, 1 in 5 people will have suicidal thoughts over the span of their lifetime, 1 in 15 attempt suicide and 1 in 14 people turn to self-harm.

Unfortunately, not everyone will understand mental health concerns such as depression and anxiety. Even fewer will understand mental health diagnoses of personality disorders and psychotic disorders such as schizophrenia or bipolar disorder. They may even doubt you have a condition or use words that make you feel dismissed or offended. If you are struggling to come to terms with this then it's important to always remember that **you are not alone**, as at times it can feel very isolating.

If you are supporting someone who has been diagnosed with a mental illness, it would be helpful to learn as much information as possible about their diagnosis, so you'll be better able to understand their feelings and emotions. Having a supportive community is very important to someone who has a mental health diagnosis, as it can be a protective factor for future relapses. If a person becomes unwell and, because of the nature of the condition, doesn't know it, then their friends, family or carers could be the first to notice the signs and encourage them to get help.

I still question myself and doubt my ability to recognise my psychotic symptoms should they return. I think I always will live with this doubt. I'm really hopeful that it will never happen to me again, but if it does then I know that I am equipped with all of the insight that I need to try to recognise it and seek help from a doctor immediately. I really highly recommend that you gain insight for yourself or your loved ones too. I hope that this book and the recommended resources can help you do so.

BRAIN HEALTH AND MENTAL HEALTH CONDITIONS

I recently listened to an episode of the *Girls Gone Bible* podcast with special guest Dr Daniel Gregory Amen. Dr Amen is a physician and psychiatrist, founder of Amen Clinics and author of books such as *Change Your Brain, Change Your Life*. I found the episode very informative and very powerful. He spoke about how doing scans of the brain is essential in the successful treatment of mental health concerns. In one of his stories, he described how cysts on the brain had been the culprit of strange behaviour, and he recounted numerous success stories where the patient was successfully treated with a whole-person and holistic approach to treatment, sometimes without the need for lifelong psychiatric medication.

Dr Amen puts the emphasis on the words 'brain health' and not the words 'mental illness'. He addresses talking therapies, diet, physical health and sleep as priority treatments, something which is often lacking in mental health institutes. In the hospital I am residing in, the food we are served is very high in starchy and refined carbohydrates, hidden sugars and additives.

They do sometimes serve fresh vegetables and fruit alongside the stodgy carbohydrates, but the bulk of the meal is not gut friendly and leaves you feeling heavy after you've finished eating. In my time in hospital, I've gained 50kg in total (starting from malnourished) but have surpassed a healthy weight by at least 20kg due to lack of nutrition and exercise. There is a gym on site with a great fitness trainer who delivers 30-minute sessions four times a week to each ward. There is also a local leisure centre nearby for people who are allowed to leave the hospital. Although there are the means to exercise here, I feel that there is not enough information and education being given surrounding the importance of exercise and nutrition for brain health.

This whole-person approach that Dr Amen speaks about should definitely be adapted by mental health facilities. The doctor has spoken on how psychiatrists can only do so much in the time allotted for them to see each patient and that unfortunately means the holistic treatment model doesn't work in mainstream psychiatry, thus leading to them heavily prescribing psychiatric medication without taking a further look into the lives and brains of each patient.

I'd highly recommend Dr Amen's book *Change Your Brain, Change Your Life*, especially if you are struggling with mental health concerns or, as he might put it, low brain health. This could be just what you need to accompany your daily dose of psychiatric medication. However, I must stress, **it's important to never come off medication without a thorough talk and plan put in place by a doctor or responsible clinician.**

BAPTISM AND HOPE IN CHRIST

In my second year in hospital, I was baptised in the local church after my realisation that I'd never be able to give up hope in Jesus. I decided that I wanted to strive to live in a way that would make God pleased and so I went through baptism to sacrifice my old ways of living and to resurrect into a new life with Jesus. It wasn't the easiest decision for me as I have a fear of water and my family were a three-hour drive away at the time, but I pushed through anyway.

With the support of an occupational therapist from the hospital, I committed my life to Jesus in a public display of faith. I read my testimony out on stage and plunged into water to become a new creation in Christ.

It was such a deeply emotional, personal experience. I know that I am changed forever because of the gospel, but even though I feel this way I still doubt myself. Sometimes I think that my experience of mental illness disqualifies me to share the gospel of Jesus. But even though I feel this way, I still try to share it. I share it because all people deserve love, forgiveness and hope. All people deserve to hear it.

I'm sure there will be people reading this who think I am crazy for believing in God and the gospel of Jesus, especially after all I've been through. Some people will think it beautiful, and others will think it just another delusion. But the truth is, I have found a faith that gives me stability in a very messy, confusing world. I have found structure, discipline, forgiveness and self-compassion. I've found instruction for a way of living that will bring me more peace than a life without that instruction. But most of all, I've found my hope. Hope in seeing the transformation that's occurring within me, hope to see it in others and a hope that I'll go to heaven to be with my loved ones once this life is over. Hope of a future and a hope of everlasting life in Christ. How could anyone ask for more than that?

PSALM 42

For the director of music. A maskil of the Sons of Korah.

>As the deer pants for streams of water,
>
>so my soul pants for you, my God.
>
>My soul thirsts for God, for the living God.
>
>When can I go and meet with God?
>
>My tears have been my food
>
>day and night,
>
>while people say to me all day long,
>
>'Where is your God?'
>
>These things I remember
>
>as I pour out my soul:
>
>how I used to go to the house of God
>
>under the protection of the Mighty One
>
>with shouts of joy and praise
>
>among the festive throng.
>
>Why, my soul, are you downcast?
>
>Why so disturbed within me?
>
>Put your hope in God,
>
>for I will yet praise Him,
>
>my Savior and my God.

My soul is downcast within me;

therefore I will remember you

from the land of the Jordan,

the heights of Hermon—from Mount Mizar.

Deep calls to deep

in the roar of your waterfalls;

all your waves and breakers

have swept over me.

By day the Lord directs His love,

at night His song is with me—

a prayer to the God of my life.

I say to God my Rock,

'Why have you forgotten me?

Why must I go about mourning,

oppressed by the enemy?'

My bones suffer mortal agony

as my foes taunt me,

saying to me all day long,

'Where is your God?'

Why, my soul, are you downcast?

Why so disturbed within me?

Put your hope in God,

for I will yet praise Him,

my Savior and my God.

PSYCHOSIS EXPLAINED

WHAT IS PSYCHOSIS?

Psychosis, also referred to as a psychotic episode or psychotic experience, is when someone perceives reality differently from other people. It may seem like someone is losing touch with reality.

The word 'psychosis' is not usually used as a diagnosis itself but is classed as an experience and is a symptom of mental health problems. People who suffer psychosis may be diagnosed with one of the following conditions:

- Schizophrenia
- Bipolar disorder
- Paranoid schizophrenia
- Schizoaffective disorder
- Severe depression
- Postpartum psychosis

SIGNS OF PSYCHOSIS

Seeing or hearing things that aren't really there (hallucinations) is a sure sign of psychosis. Believing things to be true that aren't actually true (delusions) and jumbled or confused (disordered) thinking and speech are also signs of psychosis.

HALLUCINATIONS

Hearing things that others don't hear. These are generally voices that are usually very positive or very negative and nasty. Sometimes these voices can tell a person to hurt themselves or others.

Seeing things that other people don't see. For example, seeing spiritual deities, religious figures or people's faces.

Experiencing touch sensations (tactile hallucinations) from things that aren't really there, such as a hand on one shoulder, a warm or cold breeze or a breath on the back of the neck.

Please ask for an urgent GP appointment if you or someone you know is suffering from hallucinations.

You can call 111 or get help from 111 online at **111.nhs.uk**

DELUSIONS

A delusion is a belief that isn't shared by others. It's important to note that lots of beliefs are not always shared by other people; a delusion, however, is a belief that nobody else shares and cannot be proven or shown to be true by other people's perceptions.

Delusions naturally feel one hundred percent true and very real to a person who has them. For example, you may feel like you have special superpowers and can control people's actions with your thoughts, or you may believe you are the queen or the true Messiah.

Some delusions can be very dark and very scary. You may feel threatened around certain people or believe that people are trying to control, kill or harm you. These delusions can sometimes be referred to as paranoia.

DISORGANISED SPEECH AND THINKING

Racing thoughts is when your thoughts seem to be racing so fast through your mind that they feel out of control.

Flight of ideas is when your thoughts seem to move between ideas very quickly. It can also refer to someone making links and finding meaning between things that other people don't understand.

Speaking very fast is a sign of disorganised thinking and may result in what is called a 'word salad', where words come out jumbled, which makes it hard for others to understand you.

Attention is hard to keep when suffering from disorganised thoughts, so changing the topic of conversation very quickly can be another sign that someone is experiencing this.

OVERVIEW OF WHAT IT CAN BE LIKE EXPERIENCING PSYCHOSIS

Psychosis can be very overwhelming in most cases as it directly affects your thoughts and ultimately your behaviour. It can leave you feeling scared, anxious and confused and also tired and lonely. It is a very isolating experience, feeling like the only person who is making sense of the truth when actually you are the only one not making sense. It can leave you very frustrated when people don't understand you and can make you feel misunderstood. People will often point out that your beliefs aren't true, and it can be very hard to trust the people around you.

Beliefs are usually very strong for someone experiencing psychosis and can seem really strange to other people. Some people experience seeing their relatives and believe they are talking to them, so it can seem like a positive experience to them at the time. Others will have very troubling beliefs, like mine for example, where I believed that I must die to save the world.

WHAT CAUSES PSYCHOSIS

Numerous situations can be a cause for psychosis. Here are some of the top ones:

- Severe depression
- Abuse and trauma
- Sickness and physical injury
- Childbirth
- A bereavement
- Lack of sleep
- A significant break-up
- Spiritual experiences
- Alcohol consumption
- Drug misuse
- Some medications have also been shown to cause psychosis.

TREATING PSYCHOSIS

If a person's symptoms are really severe then they may be admitted to a mental health hospital for treatment.

Psychosis can be treated with a mixture of different treatments, including antipsychotic medication, one-to-one counselling or talking therapies, cognitive behavioural therapy and compassion focused therapy, and also social support such as supported accommodation and help with social needs.

How long the treatment takes can vary from person to person and depends on the diagnosis. Some people may taper off medication completely as they come to a point where the symptoms are gone. Others may take medication long term and have to use coping strategies learned in one-to-one sessions daily to relieve themselves of and try to manage symptoms. It is important to never come off antipsychotic medication without the help and instruction of a doctor.

Dietary and lifestyle choices are also important when it comes to treating any mental health diagnosis. Things like getting enough sleep each night are imperative to brain health and function.

There is some evidence that suggests trying an elimination diet can help in reducing symptoms. More and more research is being done on the connection between gut health and brain health. By eliminating the top common allergenic foods, like dairy, gluten, corn, etc., from our diets and reintroducing them one by one, we can see if we have sensitivities to the foods. If we find we have bloating, gut sensitivities or low mood after consumption of a certain food, we should try eliminating it long term to potentially boost brain health. Eating a wholefoods diet and staying away from ultra-processed food is also beneficial for overall health.

Regular exercise (something that can be hard when you feel depressed) is also extremely important for overall health. Brain training games and keeping your brain engaged in general has been shown to improve cognitive function and slow cognitive decline in people with mental health concerns. Staying connected with friends and loved ones is also a proven way to boost chemicals such as dopamine and serotonin in the brain and keeps loneliness at bay. Loneliness has proven to be another trigger for poor mental health.

Avoiding drugs, smoking and alcohol is really important. Although drugs, smoking and alcohol may seem to help short term with the stress of a mental health condition, they are dire to your overall health. Drugs and alcohol may mask symptoms of a mental health condition or make symptoms such as hallucinations worse. **(If you live in the UK and need help refraining from alcohol or drugs, please refer to the resources at the back of this book.)**

RESOURCES FOR MORE IN-DEPTH INFORMATION ON PSYCHOSIS

www.mind.org

The best resource for mental health conditions and general mental health concerns. Really thorough explanations of psychosis, hearing voices, hallucinations and individualised mental health conditions.

www.rethink.org

Extensive resource for more advice and information on mental health conditions, how to seek help, advocacy and rights when it comes to treatment.

www.nhs.uk

Advice and information on specific mental health diagnoses and when to seek help.

www.hearing-voices.org

The Hearing Voices Network is a small charity dedicated to reducing the stigma around hearing voices. On the website you will find video resources that are very helpful in understanding voices, and short films of people's experiences with hearing voices.

CHRISTIAN/CHURCH RESOURCES

www.mindandsoulfoundation.org

Helping equip leaders to care for themselves and those that they serve.

www.betterhelp.com

Online Christian counselling services.

www.acc-uk.org

Online Christian counselling services.

GETTING HELP WITH DRUG AND ALCOHOL PROBLEMS

www.alcoholics-anonymous.org.uk

Help with alcohol problems in the UK.

www.wearewithyou.org.uk

Help and advice for people with drug and alcohol problems in the UK. Also supports friends and family.

BOOKS

Hope for Troubled Minds, Tony Roberts

Psychosis: Stories of Recovery and Hope, Jane Fradgley

Pardon My Psychosis, James Coast

Brain on Fire, Susannah Cahalan

Diagnosis: Psychosis, Olivia Russo

CBT for Dummies, Rhena Branch and Rob Wilson

Change Your Brain, Change Your Life, Daniel G. Amen

THE GOOD NEWS

God created mankind. God loves us so much that He has always had a plan to rescue us from sin and bring us home to Him. Since the beginning of time, God knew that our hearts would grow cold towards Him and we would live out our lives in separation from Him, lying, cheating and even questioning His existence. But His plan was wonderful...

This plan was to conceive a child. A child born of a virgin. A child whose biological mother was human and whose father was God Himself, thus making the child fully human and fully God.

This child wasn't just any child; this child was Jesus Christ. Jesus has always been with God since the beginning of time, waiting to be sent and born into the world for His purpose.

You see, God is triune. Meaning, God is three persons making up one God. The Father, the Son

(Jesus) and the Holy Spirit. This triune God has always been in existence and always will be in existence; He has no end and no beginning.

So here we have it, God being born on earth to a virgin named Mary and being named Jesus.

Jesus was to grow into a man before He was to make Himself known to the world as the saviour of all mankind.

He performed many miracles and healed many people; He prayed to His father unceasingly and cast out demons by the power of His own name. He created disciples of men and taught them everything they needed to know about His father's plan.

The plan was that there would come a time when Jesus would have to leave earth and return to His father in heaven. Jesus would be persecuted and put to death for calling Himself the Messiah. His own unbelieving people would persecute Him and put Him to death on a cross. This was so that the plan would be complete.

The law at the time was that blood sacrifice was to be carried out for forgiveness of sins. People sacrificed livestock to God to be cleansed of their sins. Jesus was to be the final lamb in God's plan, Jesus (God Himself) put to death on a cross as the final sacrifice for sins for good. For everyone! For sinners everywhere! No exceptions! Jesus was God's sacrificial lamb that was used as an outstretched hand to guide His people home to Him.

So, Jesus left the world with a promise to people who believe in Him.

Jesus promised that whoever believes in Him and loves Him would receive eternal life in heaven with Him. That they would receive forgiveness for all of their sins and that there would be eternal life full of love, joy and spiritual satisfaction with Jesus in heaven, after the death of their bodies here on earth.

In dying on that cross and resurrecting to eternal life, Jesus has claimed victory over sin and death and invites us to share in His victory!

After the death of Jesus, one of the women who followed Him, Mary, visited the tomb to prepare His body but when she got there she found the tomb empty.

Soon after, Jesus appeared to His disciples and showed them that He lived again; He showed them the wounds of the crucifixion still on His resurrected body. He had already told them that He is the way to heaven and that He is the truth and that they should travel and preach the truth to as many people as possible. He told them that He would send the Holy Spirit as a helper to them as they travelled the world preaching about His promise.

His promise is the same today as it was two thousand years ago. If you call on Jesus as your Lord and saviour, repent and believe in your heart that He is the truth then you will be forgiven, saved and set free. He promises to carry your burdens with you in this life and set you free for eternity in the next chapter.

Wow, isn't that the most amazing love story?

ACKNOWLEDGEMENTS

A huge, gigantic thank you to my dear psychologist, Rebecca, for encouraging me to have the strength I needed to breakdown over and over again. You provided a safe space for me to crumble and helped to build my confidence enough that I am able to start to slowly rebuild myself piece by piece. Forever grateful.

To all the amazing healthcare assistants, thank you!

Thank you to the responsible clinicians whose care I have been entrusted into, along with the rest of the medical team.

To David, the best nurse on Eden, thank you for treating me even when I refused treatment. You, frustratingly, never took no for an answer and I'm deeply grateful. When I was healing, you always offered me an ear to listen and you never rushed your kind words to me. Thank you for everything.

To the occupational therapists, thank you. Thank you for the chats and laughs and all that you've done to keep me occupied during my stay in hospital. Without working in the cafe alongside you, I would have been aimlessly moping around on my own on the ward. You gave me small purposes to motivate me. Thank you.

To Edward and Ayo, thank you for being my friends and always being ready to chat to me. It's the small things that make the biggest difference.

A massive thank you to my amazing, supportive family. Without you, I don't know where I'd be right now. I feel truly blessed to have a family that is as supportive as you. I love you.

Steph, you're amazing. You never judge me unfairly and you're always there for me through the hardest times of my life. You're honest, hardworking and funny and you're the best friend I could ever wish for. I love you.

To my sisters on the ward. I am so lucky to have shared my time in hospital with you two. From corridor chats to all the giggles we've shared, I am truly lucky to have your friendships.

To a beautiful special someone in heaven, you have always been and always will be the force behind my drive. Thank you for loving me. I love you forever and a day.

Thank you to Rethink Mental Illness for taking me on as an involvement champion. Attending meetings and sharing snippets of my story has encouraged me to write this book. Thank you for helping to build my confidence enough to share with others.

Thank you God for all you've given me and all you've provided me with. Thank you for Jesus. I am and will always be eternally grateful. I promise to thank you every day of my life!

What Did You Think of
Psychosis: A Memoir?

A big thank you for purchasing this book. It means a lot that you chose this book specifically from such a wide range on offer. I do hope you enjoyed it.

Book reviews are incredibly important for an author. All feedback helps them improve their writing for future projects and for developing this edition. If you are able to spare a few minutes to post a review on Amazon, that would be much appreciated.

Publisher Information

Rowanvale Books provides publishing services to independent authors, writers and poets all over the globe. We deliver a personal, honest and efficient service that allows authors to see their work published, while remaining in control of the process and retaining their creativity. By making publishing services available to authors in a cost-effective and ethical way, we at Rowanvale Books hope to ensure that the local, national and international community benefits from a steady stream of good quality literature.

For more information about us, our authors or our publications, please get in touch.

www.rowanvalebooks.com
info@rowanvalebooks.com

www.ingramcontent.com/pod-product-compliance
Lightning Source LLC
LaVergne TN
LVHW070013090426
835508LV00048B/3380